Cambridge Primary

Hodder Cambridge Primary

# Science

## Workbook

## Stage 1

Rosemary Feasey

Series editor: Deborah Herridge

HODDER
EDUCATION
AN HACHETTE UK COMPANY

## Acknowledgements

The Publisher is extremely grateful to the following schools for their comments and feedback during the development of this series:
Avalon Heights World Private School, Ajman
The Oxford School, Dubai
Al Amana Private School, Sharjah
British International School, Ajman
Wesgreen International School, Sharjah
As Seeb International School, Al Khoud

The publisher would like to thank the following for permission to reproduce copyright material.

**p.41** http://www.cotlands.org.za/snakes-and-ladders (Image credit: This image is believed to be in the public domain.)

Note: While every effort has been made to check the instructions for practical work described in this book carefully, schools should conduct their own risk assessments in accordance with local health and safety requirements.

Every effort has been made to trace all copyright holders, but if any have been inadvertently overlooked the Publishers will be pleased to make the necessary arrangements at the first opportunity.

Although every effort has been made to ensure that website addresses are correct at time of going to press, Hodder Education cannot be held responsible for the content of any website mentioned in this book. It is sometimes possible to find a relocated web page by typing in the address of the home page for a website in the URL window of your browser.

Hachette UK's policy is to use papers that are natural, renewable and recyclable products and made from wood grown in sustainable forests. The logging and manufacturing processes are expected to conform to the environmental regulations of the country of origin.

Orders: please contact Bookpoint Ltd, 130 Milton Park, Abingdon, Oxon OX14 4SB.
Telephone: (44) 01235 827720. Fax: (44) 01235 400454. Lines are open from 9.00–5.00, Monday to Saturday, with a 24-hour message answering service. You can also order through our website: www.hoddereducation.com

© Rosemary Feasey 2017

Published by Hodder Education

An Hachette UK Company

Carmelite House, 50 Victoria Embankment, London EC4Y 0DZ

Impression number    7

Year                 2021

Cover illustration © Steve Evans

Illustrations by Jeanne du Plessis

Typeset in FS Albert Regular 17 on 19pt by IO Publishing CC

Printed in Great Britain by Ashford Colour Press Ltd , Gosport, Hampshire

A catalogue record for this title is available from the British Library

9781471883941

# Contents

# Unit 1 Plants

## Alive or not alive?

**1** Draw a circle around the things that are alive.

**2** Draw a picture in each box. Draw:
  **a** something that is alive    **b** something that is not alive.

| alive | not alive |
|---|---|

# Find out!

**1** Look at the picture of a dandelion.
Find out if it is alive.
Tick 'yes' or 'no' to these questions.

| Question | Yes ✔ | No ✗ |
|---|---|---|
| **a** Does it grow? | | |
| **b** Does it make new dandelions? | | |
| **c** Does it need food? | | |

**2** Is a dandelion alive? Tick one box.

YES   NO

**3** Here is a picture of a kettle.

Answer these questions to find out if it is alive.
Tick 'yes' or 'no' for each.

| Question | Yes ✔ | No ✗ |
|---|---|---|
| **a** Does it grow? | | |
| **b** Does it move? | | |
| **c** Does it make new kettles? | | |
| **d** Does it need food? | | |

**4** Is a kettle alive? Tick one box.

YES   NO

# Spot the living things

 Tariq was looking for living things on his way home from school. Draw circles around the living things he saw.

# Plant parts

**1** Look at the picture of the plant.
Use these words to label the parts of the plant:

leaf    stem    flower    roots

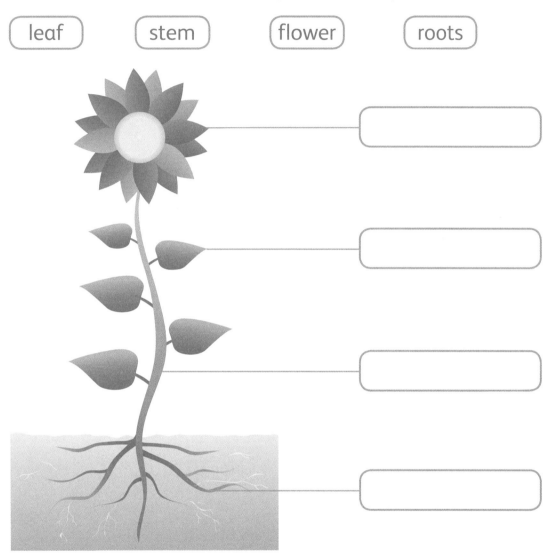

**2** Cover the words below with your hand. Try to spell each word.
You have three chances for each word. How good were you?

roots    _____  _____  _____

stem     _____  _____  _____

leaf     _____  _____  _____

flower   _____  _____  _____

# Vegetables

 Nuru's mum is making vegetable stew.
Which part of the plant is Nuru's mum using?
Draw lines to match the correct word to each vegetable.

( root )    ( stem )    ( leaves )    ( seeds )    ( flower )

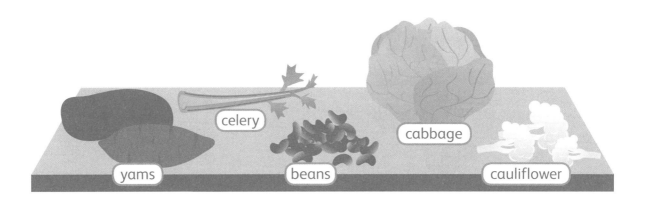

celery

cabbage

yams        beans        cauliflower

 **a** Draw three vegetables that you like in the boxes below.

|  |  |  |
|---|---|---|
|  |  |  |

_____    _____    _____

**b** Write which part of a plant they are on the lines above.
Choose from these words:

( root )    ( stem )    ( leaves )    ( seeds )    ( flower )

# Planting seeds

 Tad was planting some seeds, but he mixed up the pictures. Put the pictures in the correct order. One has been done.

 **a** Draw a picture to show that the seed has grown into a plant.

**b** Now label the parts of your plant.

## What do seeds need?

 Maya was thinking about what seeds need to grow.

Do seeds need water to grow?

Draw a picture to show what Maya could do to find out.

2 Predict what you think will happen to the seeds she plants.

I think _____

_____

# What do plants need?

 Maya had another question about plants.

Maya's teacher gave her two plants.

Do plants need light to grow?

**a** What could Maya do with the plants to find out?
Draw your idea in the box.

**b** Write a sentence to say what she should do.

_____

_____

2 Predict what you think will happen to the two plants.

I think _____

_____

# Measuring bean plants

 Rav and Rosh grew a bean plant.
They measured the plant every two days.

Here are their results.

day 1    day 3    day 5    day 7    day 9

Look at their results to answer these questions.

**a** How many cubes tall was the plant on day 3? _____

**b** How many cubes tall was the plant on day 5? _____

**c** On what day was the plant the tallest? _____

**d** On what day was the plant three cubes tall? _____

# Plant detectives

 You were a plant detective.
You looked for plants in your school grounds.

**a** Draw three plants that you found in your school grounds.

**b** Under each plant, write where you found them.

I found this plant

I found this plant

I found this plant

_____

_____

_____

 Go back to your pictures.
Label the parts of each plant you found.
Use these words:

stem      leaf      flower

# Make a model plant

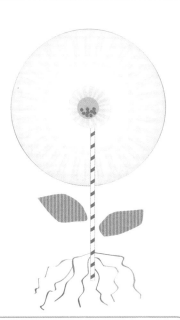

 You are going to make a model of a plant, using clean junk materials.

   **a** Draw a plan of what your model plant will look like.

   **b** What kind of materials will you use for each part of the plant?

   **c** Label the names of the parts of the plant on your drawing.

 Show your plan to a partner. Ask them to say:
  • something good about your model
  • how you could make your model better.

# Plant words

 Here are six words to do with plants. Learn how to spell them. Ask someone to test you.

1   plant

2   stem

3   leaf

4   flower

5   roots

6   tree

**2** Cora has jumbled up six words. Unjumble each word.
Use the spellings in question 1 to help you.
Write the correct word underneath:

| mste | lanpt | lfea |

_____   _____   _____

| eert | toors | rewolf |

_____   _____   _____

# Self-assessment

## Unit 1 Plants

I need more help with ...

😊 I understand this well.

😐 I understand this but need more practice.

☹ I do not understand this yet.

_____

_____

_____

_____

| Learning objectives | 😊 | 😐 | ☹ |
|---|---|---|---|
| I can say what is alive or not alive. | | | |
| I can say why plants are living things. | | | |
| I can name different parts of a plant. | | | |
| I can say what seeds need to grow. | | | |
| I know that plants need light and water to grow. | | | |
| I can name the parts of plants that I eat. | | | |
| I can find plants around the school grounds. | | | |
| I can name some of the plants in the school grounds. | | | |

# Unit 2 Ourselves

## We are the same and different

 Draw a picture of yourself.
Then draw a picture of your friend.
Use the spaces below.

a picture of yourself

a picture of your friend

**2** Look at the pictures of you and your friend.

**a** Find three things that are the same. Make a small red cross to show them.

**b** Find three things that are different. Make a small blue cross on these.

# Parts of the body

 These labels are all parts of the body.
Draw lines to the correct words to label this picture.

head

shoulder

arm

wrist

chest

knee

hand

elbow

leg

ankle

foot

 Here are some more names of body parts.

neck      chin      fingers

**a** Find out where each part is on the body.

**b** Add them to your picture.

# How tall?

 Some Stage 1 learners used string to measure their height. They stuck the strings on the wall and compared them.

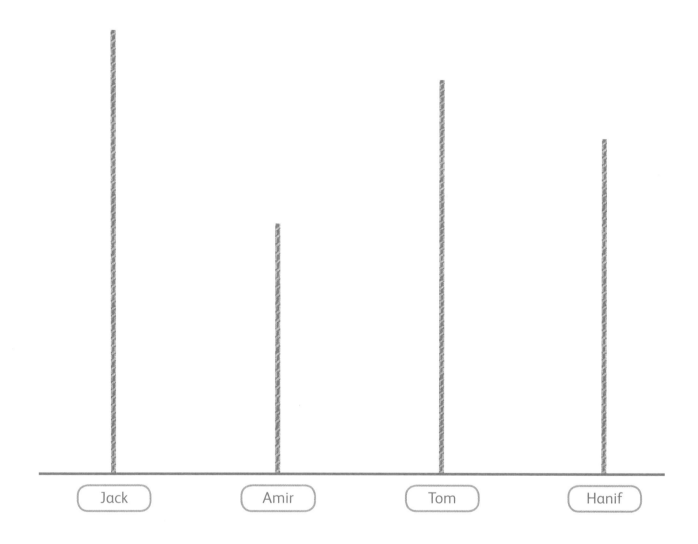

| Jack | Amir | Tom | Hanif |

a Who is the tallest? _____

b Who is the shortest? _____

c Is Tom taller than Hanif? _____

d Is Jack taller than Amir? _____

19

# Comparing heads

 Cheng and Peng used string to measure around their heads.

They used cubes to measure the string to find out how big their heads are.

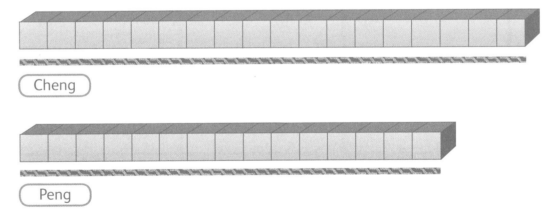

**a** How many cubes long is Cheng's string? _____

**b** How many cubes long is Peng's string? _____

**c** Who has the biggest head? _____

**d** Who has the smallest head? _____

**e** How many cubes more is the bigger head? _____

# Taller or shorter?

 **1** Are you taller or shorter than these animals?
The first one has been done for you.

**a** I am *shorter* than an elephant.

**b** I am _____ than a penguin.

**c** I am _____ than a rabbit.

**d** I am _____ than a cat.

**e** I am _____ than a giraffe.

 **2** Now write two sentences of your own.
Use the words in the boxes.

**a** ( taller than )

_____

_____

**b** ( shorter than )

_____

_____

# Where are our senses?

**1**  **a** Draw a picture of yourself.

**b** Label your senses in the correct places on the picture.

**2**  Write a sentence about what you can do with each sense. The first one has been done for you.

**a** Smell. *I can smell flowers with my nose.*

**b** Sight. _____

**c** Touch. _____

**d** Hearing. _____

**e** Taste. _____

# Our senses

 Match the correct word to the sentence.

The first one has been done for you.

| a | You use this for your sense of smell. |
|---|---|
| b | You use this for your sense of touch. |
| c | You use these for your sense of sight. |
| d | You use these for your sense of hearing. |
| e | You use this for your sense of taste. |

ears

eyes

tongue

skin

nose

**2** Write the missing parts of the eye in the correct places.
Choose from these words:

( eyebrow )　( eyelash )　( eyelid )

iris

pupil

# Spot the difference!

 Sight is one of the five senses.
Write down the names of the other four senses.

1 _____

2 _____

3 _____

4 _____

 How carefully do you look at things? Look at picture 1 and picture 2 below.

  **a** Spot how many differences you can see. There are six for you to find!

  **b** Draw a circle around all the differences you can see in picture 2.

picture 1

picture 2

# Look closely

 Scientists look closely at things.

a Use your sense of sight. What is missing from the second picture that is in the first picture?

b Draw what is missing.

c Show your drawing to a partner.

d Can your partner see anything that you have missed? What is it?

# Hand sizes

**a** Do you think your hand is bigger or smaller than your partner's hand?

_____

**b** How can you use these squares to find out? What will you do?

**c** Try your idea.

What did you find out?
Is your hand **bigger** or **smaller**?
Complete these sentences.

**a** My hand is _____ than my partner's hand.

**b** I know this because my hand is _____ squares

big. My partner's hand is _____ squares big.

# All kinds of smells

a Which smells do you like?
Which smells do you not like?

b Draw pictures of things that you like to smell and do not like to smell.

| things I like to smell  | things I do not like to smell  |
| --- | --- |
| | |

# Nice smells

 Look at the pictograph. It shows the smells that some Stage 1 learners liked. Use it to answer the questions below.

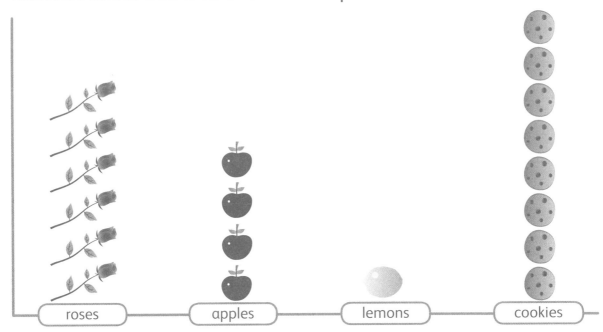

| roses | apples | lemons | cookies |

**a** How many learners liked cookies  ? _____

**b** Which smell did one learner like? _____

**c** How many learners liked roses  ? _____

**d** Did more learners like roses or apples ? _____

 **a** Draw two things that you can smell inside your house.
**b** Draw two things that you can smell outdoors.

| inside my house |
|---|
|  |

| outdoors |
|---|
|  |

# Questions about taste

 Lev has some questions to ask his partner about taste.

What is your favourite taste?

Which taste do you like more, an apple or a pear?

What taste do you like that is sour?

Ask three of your own questions.
Write each question in a speech bubble below.

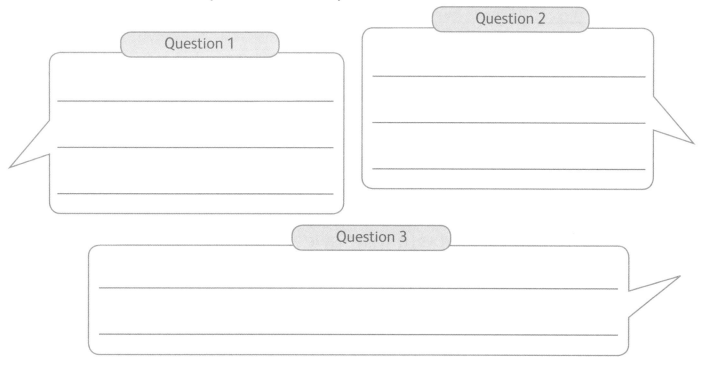

Question 1

Question 2

Question 3

 **a** Ask your partner your questions.
**b** Write the answers below.

Question 1: _____

Question 2: _____

Question 3: _____

# More about senses

**1** Use these words to complete the sentences below:

( smell )  ( nose )  ( touch )  ( salty )

( five )  ( see )  ( taste buds )

a  There are _____ senses.

b  The senses are sight, hearing, taste _____ and

_____.

c  I use my eyes to _____.

d  If you hold your _____ when you eat an apple,

you cannot taste it very well.

e  There are _____ on the tongue.

f  Taste buds help you to taste sweet, sour and

_____ tastes.

**2** Complete the sentence below. Use one of these words:

( smell )  ( sight )  ( taste )  ( hearing )  ( touch )

I think that the most important sense is _____.

This is because _____

_____

# Self-assessment

## Unit 2 Ourselves

I need more help with …

_____

_____

_____

_____

😊 I understand this well.

😐 I understand this but need more practice.

☹️ I do not understand this yet.

| Learning objectives | 😊 | 😐 | ☹️ |
|---|---|---|---|
| I can notice things that are the same or similar between me and my partner. | | | |
| I can notice things that are different between me and my partner. | | | |
| I can name parts of my body. | | | |
| I can measure my head. | | | |
| I know the names of the five senses. | | | |
| I can name the part of the body that goes with each sense. | | | |
| I can use my senses to find out things in the world around me. | | | |

# Unit 3 Living and growing

## A living thing

 Jake has a pet bird called Bluey.

What does the bird do, which tells you that it is alive?

_____

**2** Complete the sentences below. Choose from these words.

( grown )  ( moves )  ( eats )  ( breathe )

a Bluey _____ around his cage, so he is alive.

b Bluey _____ when he is hungry.

c Bluey has two holes at the top of his beak,

so he can _____.

d Jake started looking after Bluey when he was a baby.

Bluey has now _____ bigger.

# Alive and never alive

 **1** Write 'alive' or 'never alive' under each picture. The first one has been done for you.

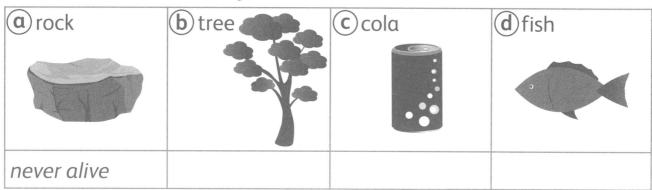

| ⓐ rock | ⓑ tree | ⓒ cola | ⓓ fish |
|---|---|---|---|
| *never alive* | | | |

| ⓔ plant | ⓕ child | ⓖ kettle | ⓗ scooter |
|---|---|---|---|
| | | | |

**2** Draw something else that is alive.

**3** Draw something else that has never been alive.

# Animal homes

 Draw a line to match the animal to its habitat.
One has been done for you.

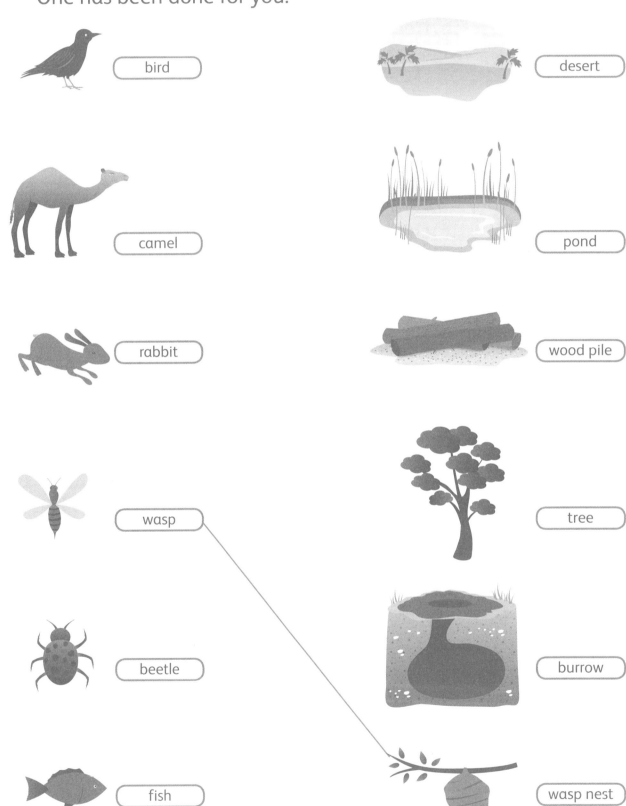

bird

desert

camel

pond

rabbit

wood pile

wasp

tree

beetle

burrow

fish

wasp nest

# Offspring

 **1** A habitat is where a plant or animal lives.
What does a habitat have so that an animal can live there?
Draw a circle around four correct words.

( cars )   ( food )   ( air )   ( people )

( shelter )   ( tea )   ( water )

**2** Match the adult animals to their offspring. One has been done.

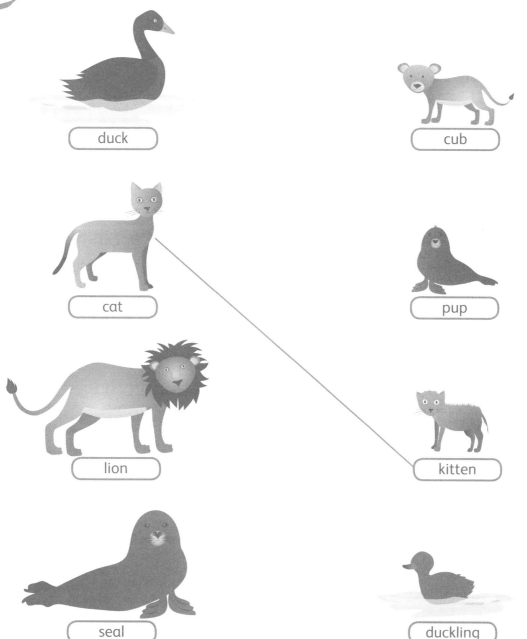

duck

cub

cat

pup

lion

kitten

seal

duckling

35

# The life cycle of a butterfly

 The pictures show the life cycle of a butterfly.
Write the number of each sentence below in the correct box.

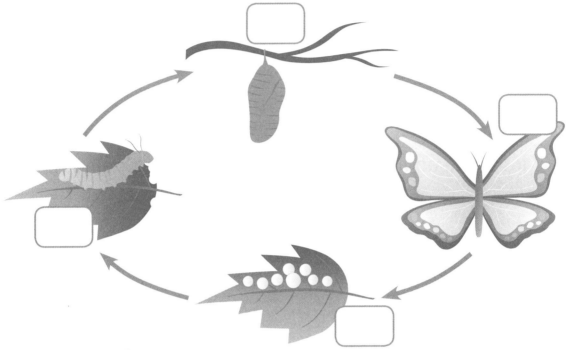

1  The butterfly lays eggs.
2  The eggs hatch into caterpillars.
3  The caterpillars make a cocoon. They change inside the cocoon.
4  The caterpillars come out of their cocoons as butterflies.

The life cycle then starts over again.

 Jazz was making a butterfly life cycle headband to wear.
But he mixed up his pictures. He drew the first picture.
Draw the other pictures in the correct order.

# Growing and changing

 As you grow up, you change. Look at these pictures.

Write something new that each person below can do as they grow up.

| A baby can |
| A toddler can |
| A school child can |
| A teenager can |
| An adult can |
| An older person can |

# Fruit and vegetables

**1** Look at these foods. Draw circles around the fruits and vegetables.

grapes    carrots    bread    okra

sweet potato    yoghurt    pasta    bananas

**2** Put a circle around the food or drink that is the least healthy.

a

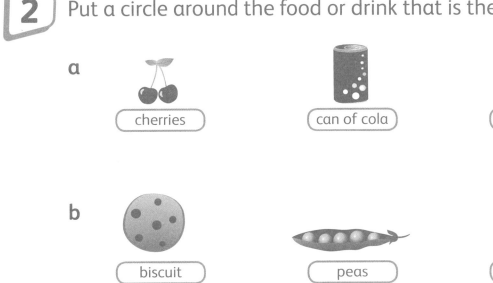

cherries    can of cola    melon

b

biscuit    peas    glass of milk

c

chocolate    apple    cheese

**3** Why are fruits and vegetables important?

_____

_____

# Food groups

**1** Draw some foods on these plates.

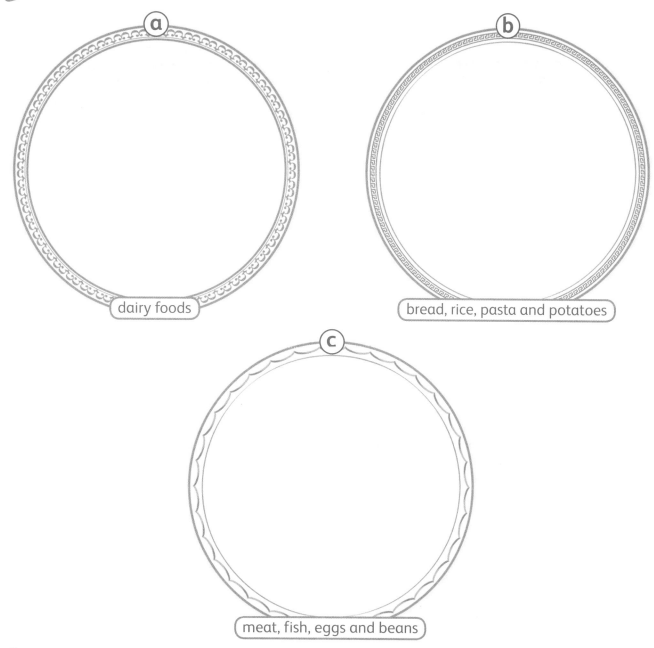

**a** dairy foods

**b** bread, rice, pasta and potatoes

**c** meat, fish, eggs and beans

**2** Choose your favourite food from each plate.

a _____

b _____

c _____

# Water diary

 Ana made a water diary.
Each day she wrote how many glasses of water and milk that she drank. She included foods that gave her water.

| | Monday | Tuesday | Wednesday | Thursday | Friday |
|---|---|---|---|---|---|
| water | | | | | |
| food | | | | | |
| milk | | | | | |

a Which day did Ana drink the most water? _____

b Which day did Ana drink the least water? _____

c Which foods did Ana eat to give her water on Thursday?

_____

d Which day did Anna drink the most milk? _____

# Down the snakes and up the ladders!

 Play this game with a partner. You will need a counter and numbers from 1 to 6 on small pieces of paper. Take turns picking a number and moving the counter from 1 to 36.

# Look after your teeth

 Jag did not look after his teeth. He had toothache. The dentist had to pull out a tooth.

**a** Draw a picture in each box to show Jag what he should do to look after his teeth.

**b** Write a sentence to go with each picture. Use these words:

( milk )  ( toothpaste )  ( toothbrush )  ( water )

| What should he do two times a day? | What should he drink? |
| --- | --- |
| | |

_____

_____

_____

_____

## Self-assessment

# Unit 3 Living and growing

I need more help with …

_____

_____

_____

_____

😊 I understand this well.

😐 I understand this but need more practice.

☹ I do not understand this yet.

| Learning objectives | 😊 | 😐 | ☹ |
|---|---|---|---|
| I can tell a partner about some things that live in the school grounds. | | | |
| I know that different plants and animals live in different places. | | | |
| I can name the offspring of some animals. | | | |
| I know how a frog and a butterfly change as they grow. | | | |
| I know how a person changes from a baby to an elderly person. | | | |
| I know different kinds of food groups. | | | |
| I can choose healthy foods from each food group to eat. | | | |
| I can say why we need to drink water. | | | |
| I know how to look after my teeth. | | | |

# Unit 4 Material properties

## Materials all around us

**1** Complete the sentences below using these words:

( material )   ( objects )

a Everything around you is made from a _____.

b All _____ are made from a material.

**2** a Look around you. Find six different objects.
   b Draw each object in a box below.
   c What material is each object made from? Write the name under the picture.

| 1 | 2 | 3 |
|---|---|---|
| material | material | material |
| 4 | 5 | 6 |
| material | material | material |

# It feels soft!

**1** Draw four objects that are made from a soft material. Write what they are.

| a | b |
|---|---|
| | |

| c | d |
|---|---|
| | |

**2** What is your favourite soft object?

My favourite soft object is _____.

45

# Material properties

 **1** Draw six objects that are made from materials that are:

( hard )  ( rough )  ( rigid )  ( soft )  ( smooth )  ( bendy )

One object has been drawn for you.

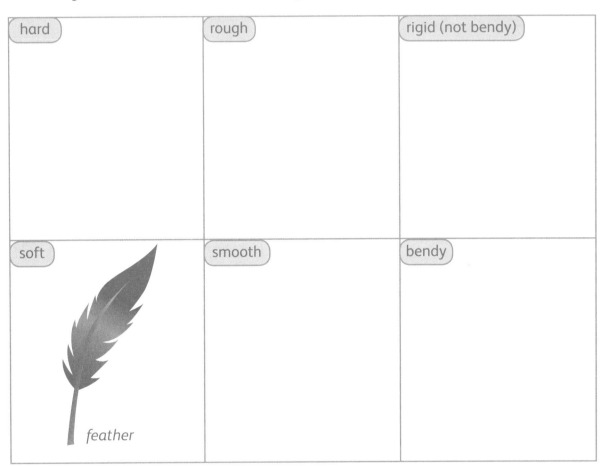

| hard | rough | rigid (not bendy) |
|---|---|---|
| soft  *feather* | smooth | bendy |

**2** Draw an object that is smooth and bendy.

( smooth and bendy )

# Opposites

 Look at the objects in each question below.
Choose the correct words in the box for each question.
Circle them.

| a | This ball is … |
|---|---|
| | bendy          rigid |
| | shiny          dull |
| | rough          smooth |
| b | This tree trunk is … |
| | bendy          rigid |
| | shiny          dull |
| | rough          smooth |
| c | This straw is … |
| | bendy          rigid |
| | shiny          dull |
| | rough          smooth |

# Materials in the kitchen

**a** Look at all the objects in the picture below.

**b** Draw an arrow pointing to each object. Then write what it is made from. One has been done for you.

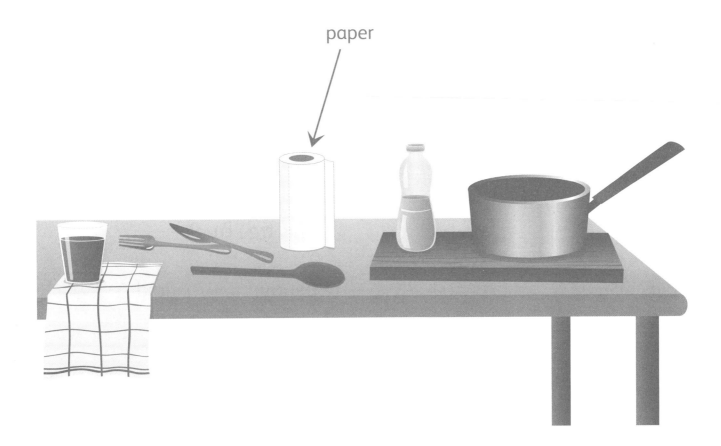

paper

2 Name one object in your kitchen that is made from each of the materials below.

**a** metal _____

**b** glass _____

**c** plastic _____

**d** fabric _____

# Metal objects

**1**

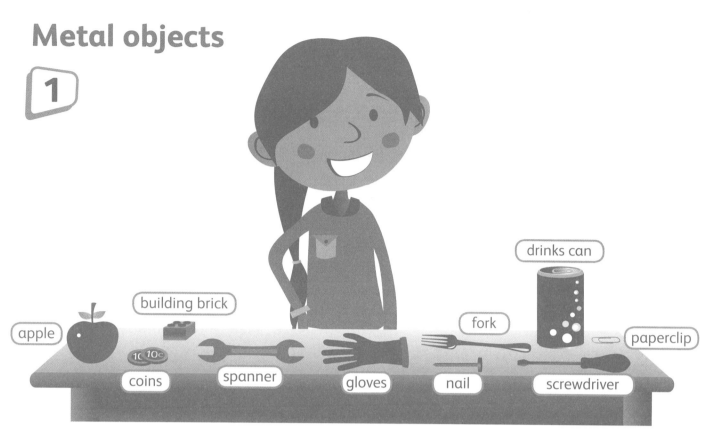

Riya collected some metal objects.

**a** Look at the objects. Which objects are not made from metal?

**b** Draw them here.

**2** Which words say what most metal materials are like?
Draw a circle around each word.

furry    hard    fluffy    shiny    cold to touch    hot to touch

# Plastic and wood

 Look around your classroom.
  a Find objects that are made from plastic.
  b Find objects that are made from wood.
  c Draw the objects in these boxes.

| made from plastic | made from wood |
|---|---|
|  |  |

 What objects do you have in your home that are made from plastic? Write three objects below.

Hint: Think about the different rooms in your home.

a _____

b _____

c _____

# Glass

 Read each sentence in the table.
Tick (✔) True or False.

| Sentence | True | False |
|---|---|---|
| **a** Glass can break. | | |
| **b** Glass is soft. | | |
| **c** Glass can be transparent (see through). | | |
| **d** All glass is red. | | |

**2** Think about your home. Draw four objects in your home that are made from glass.

# Which material stretches the most?

**1** Fabrics are useful.
The clothes you wear are often made from stretchy fabrics.
Your clothes stretch on your body so that you can run and play.

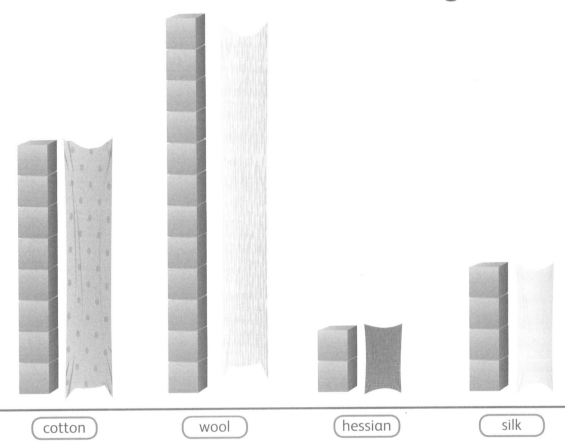

cotton          wool          hessian          silk

Look at the pictograph. Then answer these questions.

**a** How many blocks did the cotton fabric stretch? _____

**b** Which fabric stretched the most? _____

**c** How many blocks did the silk fabric stretch? _____

# Different fabrics

 Riya found some fabrics. She cut them up and stuck them into the table below. She explored what they were like.
Here is what she found out.

| Fabric | What it was like |
|---|---|
| cotton | thin<br>smooth<br>stretchy |
| hessian | thick<br>rough<br>strong |
| wool | soft<br>warm |

What fabrics should Riya use to make the objects shown here?
The first one has been done for you.

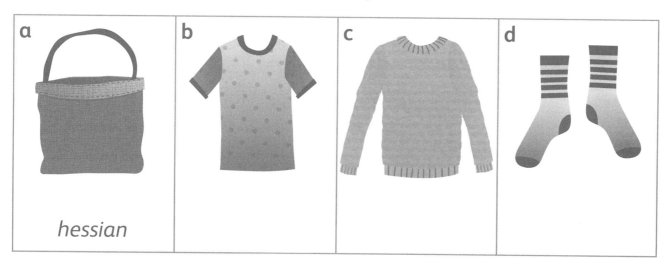

a *hessian*

b

c

d

# My clothes

 **a** Draw a picture of yourself in your favourite clothes.

**b** Label the different materials that your clothes are made from. Do not forget your shoes.

**c** Draw a circle around any materials that are waterproof.

**2** Draw two things you can wear that are made from waterproof materials.

# Mopping up spills

 A Stage 1 class tested materials to find out which material is best for mopping up juice. They predicted that a sponge would mop up all of the juice. Here is a table of their results.

| Material | What happened |
|---|---|
| paper towel | mopped up juice but the table was sticky |
| cloth | mopped up all of the juice |
| sponge | mopped up some of the juice |
| plastic bag | did not mop up any juice |

Look at the table. Use it to answer these questions.

**a** Which material was best for mopping up? _____

**b** Which material did not mop up any juice? _____

**c** Was their prediction correct? _____

# On the way to school

**What did you see on the way to school?**

**a** Draw four things you saw in the boxes below.

**b** Name the material each thing was made from.

I saw a _____

It was made from _____

I saw a _____

It was made from _____

I saw a _____

It was made from _____

I saw a _____

It was made from _____

# Self-assessment

## Unit 4 Material properties

I need more help with ...

☺ I understand this well.

😐 I understand this but need more practice.

☹ I do not understand this yet.

_____

_____

_____

_____

| Learning objectives | ☺ | 😐 | ☹ |
|---|---|---|---|
| I can say what different materials feel like. | | | |
| I can say what different materials look like. | | | |
| I can sort materials into groups. | | | |
| I can say if objects are soft, hard, rough or smooth. | | | |
| I can name different materials. | | | |
| I know what fabrics can be used for. | | | |
| I can explore materials to find out what they are like. | | | |
| I can compare different materials. | | | |

## Unit 5 Forces

## How things move

 Things move in different ways.
Match the pictures to the correct words.
The first one has been done for you.

| | |
|---|---|
| | slither |
| | crawl |
| | swim |
| | roll |
| | run |
| | fly |
| | hop |

# Twisting, stretching and squashing

**1** What is happening in the pictures below? Use these words:

( twisting )    ( stretching )    ( squashing )

**a** This boy is

_____ his legs.

**b** These hands are

_____ the dough.

**c** These hands are

_____ the scarf.

**2** Draw a picture of something else you can twist, stretch or squash.

# Pushes and pulls

**1** Complete the sentences below.
Use these words: pull          push

    **a** When you _____, you make an object
move away from you.

    **b** When you _____, you make an object
move towards you.

**2** Do you use a push or a pull to move the objects below?
Could you use both? Put a tick ✔, a cross ✗ or both.
One has been done for you.

| Object | Push to move | Pull to move |
|---|---|---|
| door | | |
| swing | | |
| doorbell | ✔ | |
| shopping trolley | | |
| toy | | |

# Skittles

 Look at this picture of Ashi playing skittles.

What happens when you play skittles?
Complete the sentences below. Use these words:

pushes          rolls          bigger

a The ball _____ on the ground.

b When the ball hits the skittles, it _____ the
skittles over.

c When the ball hits one skittle, that skittle

_____ the other skittles over.

d A _____ push can knock down more skittles.

# Squirty bottle forces

 Some Stage 1 learners found out more about forces.

They used plastic bottles to squirt water onto a ball.

Then they counted bricks to see how far the ball moved.

Here are their results.

| Name | Number of bricks to show how far the ball moved |
|------|--------------------------------------------------|
| Peter | 6 bricks |
| Anna | 15 bricks |
| Josh | 10 bricks |
| Riyah | 8 bricks |

a Who pushed the ball the furthest with the squirty bottle?

_____

b Who pushed the ball 10 bricks? _____

c Who came last? _____

d Who used the biggest push with the squirty bottle?

_____

e Who used the smallest push? _____

# Pushing and pulling

**1** Complete the sentences below. Use these words:

( pushing )     ( pulling )

**a** The girl is

_____ the kite.

**b** What will she have to do to change the direction of the kite?

_____

_____

**c** The boy is

_____ the ball.

**d** What will he have to do to change the direction of the ball?

_____

_____

**e** The family is

_____ the rope.

**f** What will they have to do to change the direction of the rope?

_____

_____

63

# Paper ball race

 A Stage 1 class had a race to find out what they could use to make a paper ball move the furthest.

Look at what they used and what they found out.

straw

They blew through the straw.

paper fan

They moved the paper fan up and down.

newspaper

They moved the newspaper up and down.

battery fan

They held the fan in front of the ball.

**a** Which object pushed the paper ball the furthest?

_____

**b** Which object pushed the paper ball four bricks?

_____

**c** How far did the straw push the paper ball?

_____

**d** Which object would you use to win the race? Why? _____

_____

# Playing with bubbles

 Look at the picture. Do you remember blowing bubbles?

Complete the sentences below using these words:

( direction )    ( blow )    ( pushes )    ( harder )    ( force )

a   To make a bubble, you _____ air into

the wand.

b   To make the bubbles bigger, you blow _____.

You use a bigger _____.

c   The wind _____ the bubbles.

d   To make the bubbles change _____, move

the wand up and down.

# How I use forces

**1** Draw a picture for each sentence in the boxes below.

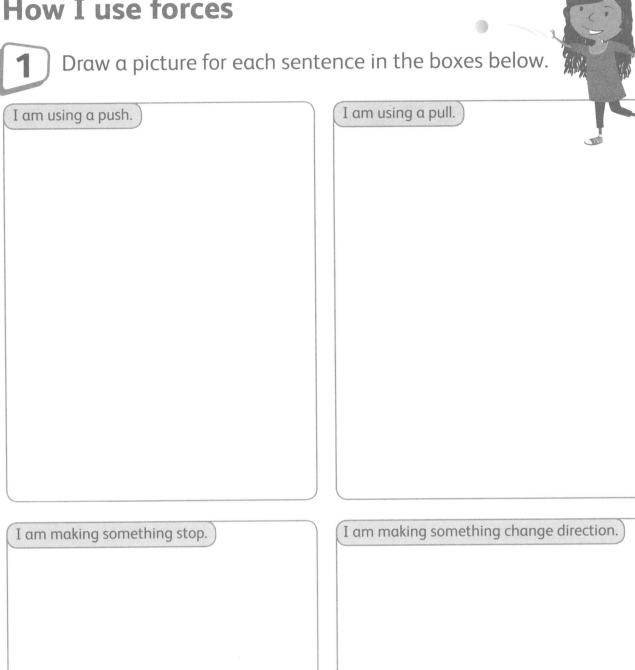

| I am using a push. | I am using a pull. |
| --- | --- |

| I am making something stop. | I am making something change direction. |
| --- | --- |

# Self-assessment

## Unit 5 Forces

I need more help with ...

🙂 I understand this well.

😐 I understand this but need more practice.

🙁 I do not understand this yet.

| Learning objectives | 🙂 | 😐 | 🙁 |
|---|---|---|---|
| I can describe how some objects move. | | | |
| I can say what a pull is. | | | |
| I can say what a push is. | | | |
| I can say what forces you use when you squash, squeeze, stretch or pull an object. | | | |
| I can name some objects you have to push to make them move. | | | |
| I can name some objects you have to pull to make them move. | | | |
| I know how to stop an object from moving. | | | |
| I know how to make an object speed up. | | | |
| I know how to make an object change direction. | | | |

## Sounds that I do not like

**1**  **a** In each box below, draw a sound that you do NOT like.

  **b** Why do you not like the sounds?
Write a sentence under each drawing.

# Sources of sound

 Draw a line to match the correct sound to each picture.

| |
|---|
| roar |
| tick tock |
| bang |
| buzz |
| meow |

**2** Draw a source of sound in each box. Write the name in the space. The first one has been done for you.

A *drum* is a source of sound.

A _____ is a source of sound.

A _____ is a source of sound.

A _____ is a source of sound.

# Making sounds

**1** Look at these pictures.
What must you do to make the instrument make a sound?
Use these words to help you:

blow    hit    pluck    shake

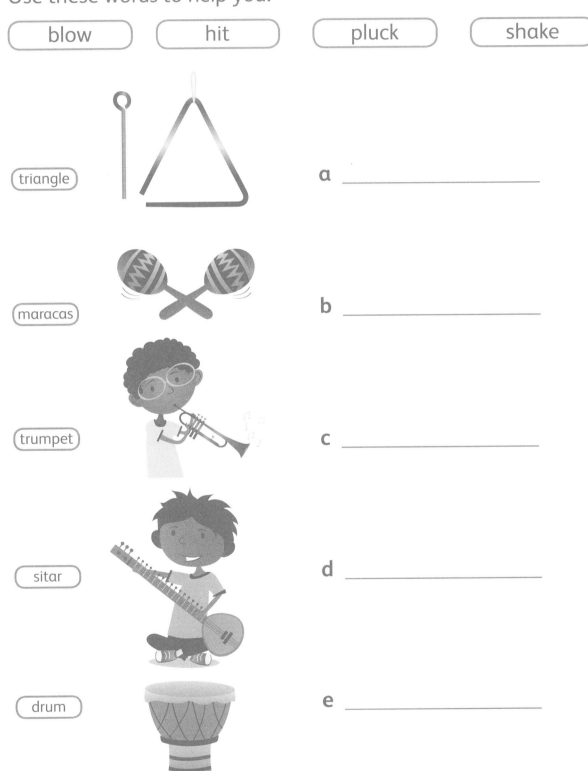

triangle    a _____

maracas    b _____

trumpet    c _____

sitar    d _____

drum    e _____

# Amazing sounds

**1** Imagine that you have an amazing bag for sounds.
   **a** Which sounds would you put into your bag?
   **b** Would they be sounds you like or sounds you do not like?
   **c** Draw and write the names of the sounds that you put into your bag.

# Sound boxes

 **1** Jed and Yash made sound boxes.

They put different objects into their boxes.
Then they shook them to make different sounds.
Here are some objects they used:

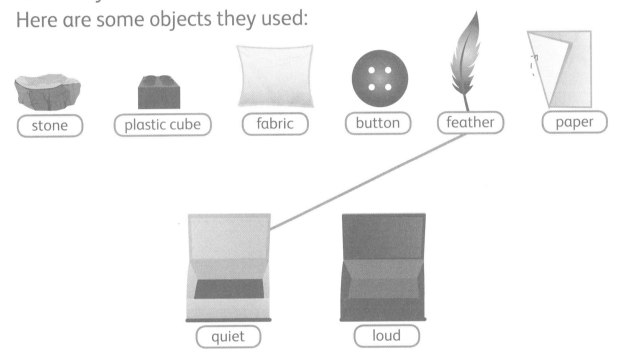

stone    plastic cube    fabric    button    feather    paper

quiet    loud

Draw a line from each object to the correct box.
The first one has been done for you.

**2** Draw four more objects that Jed and Yash could put into their sound boxes. The objects must make interesting sounds when they shake the box.

# What can you hear?

**1** Sit quietly.
What sounds can you hear? Draw and label two sources of sound in the boxes.

| I can hear _____. | I can hear _____. |

**2** Predict what will happen to the sounds if you put your hands over your ears and listen.

I predict that _____

_____

**3** Loud sounds are dangerous because _____

_____

**4** Are these sentences true or false? Put a ring around T or F.
  **a** Animals have big ears so that they can hear better. (T) (F)
  **b** Humans do not have ears. (T) (F)
  **c** If you wear earmuffs the sound will be louder. (T) (F)
  **d** People wear earmuffs to stop sound hurting their ears. (T) (F)

# Looking after your ears

**1** Here are some ways to look after your ears.
Draw a picture in the box under each sentence.

**a** Keep your ears clean by washing them when you wash your face.

**b** Never put anything unsafe into your ears.

**c** Never shout in the ear of another person. It could hurt them.

# Using a stethoscope

**1** What sound can the doctor hear?

_____

_____

_____

**2** You made your own stethoscope.
What sound did you hear when you used it?

_____

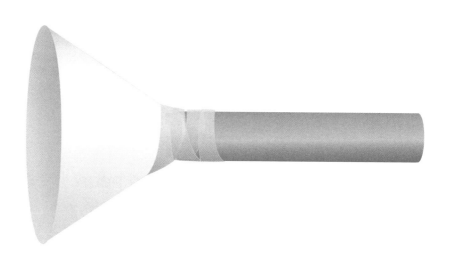

**3** What was the source of the sound you heard when using
your stethoscope?

_____

# Sounds near and far

 **1** Chen made some sounds. Ting listened to find out which object she could still hear 20 steps away.

Here is what they found out.

| Object | Could Ting hear it? |
|---|---|
| feather shaker | no |
| tambourine | yes |
| cymbals | yes |

| Object | Could Ting hear it? |
|---|---|
| whistle | yes |
| tapping sticks | no |

**a** Which sources of sound could Ting hear?

_____

**b** Which sources of sound could Ting not hear?

_____

**c** What could Chen do with the tapping sticks so that Ting will hear them?

_____

# Sounds getting fainter

 Class 1 wanted to find out how far away they could hear sounds.

One learner hit a drum while the other learners walked away.

They stopped when they could not hear the drum.

They made a chart to show what happened.

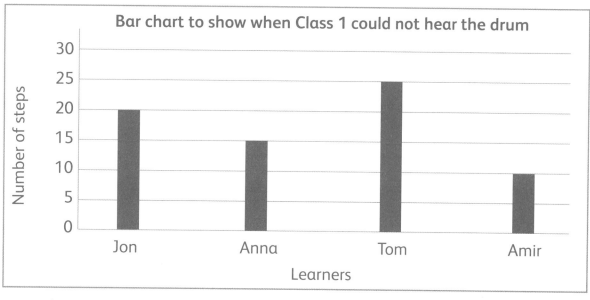

Use the chart to answer these questions.

a  Who could hear the drum the furthest away?

_____

b  How many steps did Jon take until he could not hear the drum?

_____

c  Draw a picture of what Class 1 did.

# Sound words

 **1** Here are some sound words. They describe a sound.

    **a** Under each word, draw a picture to show the source of the sound. The first one has been done for you.

| quack | howl | hiss | buzz |
|---|---|---|---|
| *duck* | | | |
| fizz | tick | pop | clap |
| | | | |
| hoot | ring | crunch | click |
| | | | |
| | | | |

    **b** Write your own sound words in the empty boxes above. Draw a picture for each word.

# Sound poem

 Complete the sound poem below.
Choose from these words:

( clock )  ( chick )  ( duck )  ( bell )  ( car )

  Quack Quack goes the _____

  Chirp Chirp goes the _____

  Brmm Brmm goes the _____

  Ring Ring goes the _____

  Tick tock goes the _____

What a lot of noise!

 Write your own sound poem.

_____

_____

_____

_____

What a lot of noise!

# Self-assessment

## Unit 6 Sound

I need more help with …

_____

_____

_____

_____

😊 I understand this well.

😐 I understand this but need more practice.

☹ I do not understand this yet.

| Learning objectives | 😊 | 😐 | ☹ |
|---|---|---|---|
| I know that hearing is one of our five senses. | | | |
| I know that we hear with our ears. | | | |
| I know that things that make a sound are called sources of sound. | | | |
| I can name some sources of sound. | | | |
| I know how to stop sound getting to our ears. | | | |
| I can tell someone how to look after their ears. | | | |
| I know that a sound gets fainter as it travels away from a source. | | | |